HUMAN RELATIONSHIPS

JACK DOMINIAN

HUMAN
RELATIONSHIPS

A short introduction

 St Paul Publications

Cover: photo by L. Lee; artwork by Mary Lou Winters FSP

Photos: Epipress pp 12, 30, 48
       Mary Lou Winters pp 36, 44, 58, 70
       Lawrence Sala pp 22, 40, 54, 64

St Paul Publications
Middlegreen, Slough SL3 6BT, England

Copyright © St Paul Publications 1989

Typeset by Grove Graphics, Tring
Printed by the Society of St Paul, Slough

ISBN 085439 288 2

St Paul Publications is an activity of the priests and brothers of the Society of St Paul who proclaim the Gospel through the media of social communication

Contents

Introduction

Studies of primitive societies indicate that human relationships are often limited to sexual intercourse which serves the physical needs of men and women and the continuation of that particular community. In these societies men and women often pursue different objectives, with the former being responsible for the material sustaining of the family and the latter carrying out the domestic work. There is little evidence of intimacy, personal feelings and affection. The men may have more than one wife, be promiscuous; the women remain under the authority of their husband, and the children be treated indifferently, with much infant mortality. In these situations love is not often a pronounced characteristic.

The concept of love is not confined to the Judaeo-Christian tradition, but it is there that it has found its most powerful advocacy. When Jesus was asked which is the first of all the commandments he replied:

"The first is this, 'Hear, O Israel: The Lord our God, the Lord is one;

and you shall love the Lord your God with all your heart, and with all your soul, and with all your mind, and with all your strength.' The second is this, 'You shall love your neighbour as yourself.' ''

Jesus makes it absolutely clear that loving is the greatest human achievement. Later on in his first Epistle John reveals that the nature of God is love.

Thus in the Christian life loving is the nearest and fullest experience of living the life of God. In fact, the twin pursuits of prayer and love sum up the Christian life. When we love our neighbour we not only fulfil God's commandment but we act in a way that everybody understands. It is no exaggeration to say that every moment of genuine loving in our life is the greatest advertisement for the presence of God.

It is a paradox but the man who has contributed most to our modern understanding of love is Sigmund Freud who was not a believer. He saw clearly that the origins of love were to be found in the child-parent relationship. All we know about love is learned in the first few years of life when parents, most often the mother, handle the baby with care, tenderness, empathy and devotion. These are the first ingredients of love we acquire and they are learned in the setting of the mother-child relationship. It is because of our deepening understanding of love in the setting of childhood that human relationships have assumed such importance in contemporary Western societies. *What is learned in childhood becomes the basis of our potential for loving throughout the rest of our life.* Whenever we experience an intimate relationship, we repeat the love we learned as a child, and that love sensitises us to love the whole world. Thus love, expressed in interpersonal relationships between parent and infant, brothers and sisters, husband and wife, friends and all our neighbours, is the highest pinnacle of human achievement and allows us to enter the very being of the Godhead.

In this small book no attempt is made to cover a wide range of love in human relationships. In the first chapter the elements that govern human relationships are outlined. Relationships are carried out by men and women who belong to a particular culture and do so with their bodies, minds and feelings. In the second an outline is given of the development of the human personality in which the roots of love are laid down. Childhood comes to an end in adolescence which is a crucial period of transition between childhood and adulthood, and the cycle of human relationships is continued with the establishment of a second intimate relationship in marriage. Marriage does not end the possibility of interpersonal relationships with the single most important alternative to be found in friendships. In both marriage and friendship men and women seek sustaining, healing and growth and the features of these elements of love are outlined in chapter 6. The most important contribution of psychology to understanding love in human relationships is to be found in the trait of self-esteem, and that is covered in chapter 7. Finally, a short account is given of some common difficulties in human relationships.

It is my hope that this booklet will be read widely and with the help of the questions at the end will start as many people as possible thinking deeply on the relationship of love and human relationships which is at the heart of being human and reflecting the image of God in men and women.

J. DOMINIAN

Chapter 1

What is relationship?

When we think of the idea of relationship, the family and its members come immediately to mind. Most of us have lived in a relationship with our mother and father, brother, sister and other relatives. The concept suggests intimacy and, indeed, it is in the family that we first learned the rudiments of love, affection, tenderness, loyalty, anger, conflict, forgiveness and reconciliation. All these experiences occur between persons in close proximity to each other. Men and women however greet, speak, touch, admire, respect, obey, work with each other on less intimate terms. In both instances they do so following their cultural, social, physical, emotional, intellectual and spiritual characteristics. The richness of human relationships is a reflection of the infinite variety of ways of communicating with each other according to the norms within which we have been brought up. It is absolutely true that the common denomination is our humanity,[but we are all different and each relationship is unique. It is this

that contributes to our significance and the basis of our faith because, ultimately, we believe that God is so full of love that he endows each one of us and our relationships with his special and personal care.⁊

Culture

Television is an excellent medium to remind us that the world is inhabited by different races, ethnic groups, with different religious and personal habits. In our own country we may be living in a community that has members from overseas. Whilst we all share the same anatomy, the differences are many and distinct. Dress, food and recreation vary enormously. Colour separates black from white and that can be accompanied by marked prejudices which are hard to eliminate. The most distinct characteristic is language, making contact with foreigners very difficult.

All these are external characteristics. But there are, of course, internal features that are cultural. The baby enters into its world, not only with different colour but markedly differentiated customs. It will receive its own unique religious upbringing, acquire family traditions that may require special filial respect and obedience to parents; many have special habits of courtship in which boys and girls do not meet except with parental consent and after marriage the wife may be expected to obey her husband to a degree no longer practised in the West.

Those of us who are born and bred in the West take our traditions for granted but, even here, there are cultural differences of language, dialect, aesthetics, habits, although increasingly there is a uniformity which allows an enormous amount of intermixing.

Thus culture is one of the most distinguishing features which shapes our interaction with others through the symbols of colour, language, gestures, dress, habits and religion. It not only forms the background of unity, but is a powerful source of conflict as the situation in Ireland and other parts of the world show.

Physical

Before we are born into the setting of a particular culture we spend nine months in the womb. This is an experience that accustoms us to closeness, warmth and the sensation of touch. When we are born we are held, stroked, kissed, fed, clothed, changed. The body is the recipient of the most powerful gestures of intimacy and communication.

Within days, and certainly weeks, of being born we begin to relate physically with our mother. We do this by holding and being held. The world of touch plays an essential role in our physical and emotional security. Beyond touch we use our eyes to track the whereabouts of mother. As a baby we first focus on her face and gradually on the rest of her body and her physical presence is a source of immense security and familiarity. Finally we begin to distinguish her voice from the earliest moment of our life and it is its softness or harshness that gives us the first intimations of feeling good or bad. Thus it is through vision, sound and touch that we form the first bonds of attachment and it is these three media that give us the vital awareness of being recognised, wanted and loved. Subsequently we shall form friendships on the basis of recognising someone as a person we like, reinforced by hearing their familiar voice. Ultimately we fall in love with someone who attracts us visually, whose voice we want to hear repeatedly and whose body we want to celebrate in and through touch.

The body is not only the principal

medium through which contact is made with another person; it is also a powerful means through which closeness or distance is maintained. The young baby needs the constant attention and proximity of mother. When mother disappears, the baby feels alone and lonely. Its immediate response is to cry and this distress signal usually brings mother back. Between the ages of three and four, the child can leave mother's side and venture into an infant school for a whole morning. It no longer needs her immediate presence. It can cope with a certain degree of aloneness without feeling lonely. It is true that at this stage the child is not entirely alone; just apart from mother, but gradually — as it gets older — it can cope with being entirely alone without feeling lonely.

In human relationships this balance of closeness and distance, aloneness and loneliness, is fundamental. Some men and women cannot bear their own company and others prefer isolation, as in some strict religious communities, explorers who navigate the seas alone for months.

But aloneness may not always be a choice of preference. Some men and women find physical intimacy very threatening and stay away from others.

These are vulnerable people who find social, physical and sexual relationship difficult. They are not always single people; they may be married and still find intimacy difficult, which leads to problems in the marriage.

Emotional

So far we have encountered the body as a basic instrument of the person, relating physically to others according to cultural norms of the individual. The body of the infant, however, is the recipient of a multitude of feelings. When the baby is interacting with mother and father it FEELS recognised, wanted and appreciated. These feelings come from the mother whose voice and touch is soft, who conveys tenderness in her voice and who smiles. The baby begins to identify these signals as affective experiences. It feels good, comfortable, loveable, wanted and appreciated. The good feelings, which are donated by the parents, becomes the child's permanent repertoire of its good sensations. As it grows older, these affirmative feelings will be experienced as a response to its behaviour.

Positive signals are not the only ones which the child hears. Mother shouts, disapproves, looks cross and the feelings are those of being temporarily cut off, bad, out of favour and unloved. In due course these negative feelings will be associated with shame and guilt and so, from a very early age, we become familiar with approval and disapproval.

At the heart of human relationships are to be found feelings of being loveable or not and part of the negative range includes anger, aggression, jealousy, envy and ultimately hate. This inner world of feelings is supremely important in human relationships.

We want to be loved and we dislike our anger and that of others. We need to feel we belong and we get anxious when our relationships are threatened by third parties who wish to displace us, making us feel jealous of our friends' and spouses' close relationships.

The importance of this inner world of feelings was not lost on our Lord who said:

> "Hear and understand: not what goes into the mouth defiles a man, but what comes out of the mouth, this defiles a man." The disciples came and said to him, "Do you

know that the Pharisees were offended when they heard this saying?" He answered, "Every plant which my heavenly Father has not planted will be rooted up. Let them alone; they are blind guides. And if a blind man leads a blind man, both will fall into a pit." But Peter said to him, "Explain the parable to us." And he said, "Are you also still without understanding? Do you not see that whatever goes into the mouth passes into the stomach, and so passes on? But what comes out of the mouth proceeds from the heart, and this defiles a man. For out of the heart come evil thoughts, murder, adultery, fornication, theft, false witness, slander. These are what defile a man; but to eat with unwashed hands does not defile a man."

(Matthew 15:10-20)

Sexual

The human dimension that everyone knows about is the attraction of the sexes and the most powerful emotion is a combination of love with the erotic. For many Christians sexuality is still a powerful but embarrassing experience and there is very little in theology which makes us celebrate this central event in our life. The fact is that the whole of humanity is dominated by sexual differences which ultimately lead to sexual attraction, marriage and sexual intercourse.

From the point of view of the development of sexuality, there are two aspects that need to be considered. The first is connected with gender. From the very start of life, little boys and girls are distinguished by the colour of their dress, the toys they are given, the games they play, the way they speak and interact and the things that engage their attention. Boys don't play with dolls and girls hardly ever entertain themselves with trains. These gender differences continue throughout childhood and form our earliest memories which distinguish the sexes. Later on psychologists find that, although the intelligence of both sexes is similar, women are more gifted in verbal abilities and men in mechanical.

The Feminist movement has rebelled violently against the idea that there is any deep-seated biological quality that dooms women to inferiority in society and the home and has considered all the inequalities as cultural. There is little doubt that a great deal of what has been attributed to the feminine role and gender is culturally determined, can be and is being changed, but there is a female chromosome and all biological differences cannot be eliminated.

The second characteristic of sexuality is the erotic dimension. The young baby and child is endowed with the capacity to feel attracted to mother through vision, sound and touch. These are affective attachments of pleasure, joy, comfort and tenderness which exists between parents and children and siblings.

Up to puberty boys and girls relate to each other on the basis of this affection. At puberty, when the secondary sexual characteristics are developed, the same means of attachment, vision, sound and touch are now endowed with erotic feelings. The young girl is now a person whose body stirs up sexual feelings. These sexual feelings do not exist for the parents and sexual molestation by parents of their children is abnormal. The sexual attraction is orientated in the vast majority of instances towards somebody of the opposite sex and occasionally towards someone of one's own sex.

This attraction is first and foremost physical and the Song of Songs, written some two and a half thousand years ago, gives us an immensely rich example of what men and women feel for one another.

This is the cry of the man:

> Behold you are beautiful, my love,
>   behold, you are beautiful!
> Your eyes are doves behind your
>   veil.
> Your hair is like a flock of goats,
>   moving down the slopes of Gilead.
>
> Your teeth are like a flock of shorn
>   ewes that have come up from the
> washing, all of which bear twins,
>   and not one among them is bereaved
> Your lips are like a scarlet thread,
>   and your mouth is lovely.
> Your cheeks are like halves of a
>   pomegranate
>   behind your veil.
> Your neck is like the tower of David,
>   built for an arsenal, whereon hang
> a thousand bucklers, all of them
>   shields of warriors.
> Your two breasts are like two fawns,
>   twins of a gazelle, that feed among
>   the lilies.

(Song of Songs 4:1-5)

And here is the reply:

My beloved is all radiant and ruddy,
  distinguished among ten thousand.
His head is the finest gold;
  his locks are wavy,
  black as a raven.
His eyes are like doves
  besides springs of water,
bathed in milk,
  fitly set.
His cheeks are like beds of spices,
  yielding fragrance.
His lips are lilies,
  distilling liquid myrrh.
His arms are rounded gold,
  set with jewels.
His body is ivory work,
  encrusted with sapphires.
His legs are alabaster columns,
  set upon bases of gold.
His appearance is like Lebanon,
  choice as the cedars.
His speech is most sweet,
  and he is altogether desirable.
This is my beloved and this is my
  friend O daughters of Jerusalem.
          (Song of Songs 5:10-16)

Beyond the contemplation of physical beauty there is a desire for intense closeness, mediated by a good deal of loving affirmation and concluded in sexual intercourse. This is all confirmed in one sentence of Genesis:

> Therefore a man leaves his father and his mother and cleaves to his wife, and they become one flesh.
>
> (Genesis 2:24)

Intellectual

In the Song of Songs the women proclaim the man's conversation is sweetness itself. In human relationships speech plays a vital role well exemplified when we are in a foreign country whose language we do not comprehend.

The child begins to acquire the capacity for speech around the second year and thereafter uses verbal abilities to communicate its inner world. We have already seen that a crucial part of that communication is concerned with feelings.

Another vital characteristic is concerned with reason. When we talk to one another we understand each other because we use the rules of language. These rules are not only concerned with grammar but with attempting to express what is rational and logical.

The whole of Western tradition has been concerned with conveying reason and we all spend some ten to fifteen years learning the logic of mathematics, language, literature, history, geography, religion and other subjects.

Before the advent of psychology in the last hundred years, the rule of reason was considered to be the supreme value in human relationships. Even today, as we listen to someone speaking, we judge whether they are clear, precise, concise, intelligent, articulate, thoughtful, wise, all of which we sum up with the idea of their rationality.

Rationality implies far more than verbal accuracy. The great Swiss psychologist, Piaget, carried out extensive tests to evaluate the growing capacities of children in their abilities with words, ideas, both concrete and abstract, visuospatial orientation, thought, memory, ability to choose colour, calculate, evaluate and many other cognitive qualities. All this comes under the heading of reason and plays a central role in human communication. In fact, men and women put so much emphasis on their reasoning that the commonest idea of madness is the loss of one's reason.

Everyone looking at the birth of a baby, following it during its growth in the next twenty years, through courtship and marriage, sexual intercourse and the bringing of a new life — thus completing the cycle — is confronted by a marvellous mystery of creation.

There are biologists who want to explain this mystery by the process of evolution with man developing as a result of billions of years of growth through the principles of genetic mutation and natural selection, spanning the interaction of molecules to the advent of men and women.

This line of humanistic thought does not answer how the first two particles from which the whole development started came into being. The need of a beginning seems inescapable. The biologist who can only answer partially the question of "how?" cannot begin to formulate the answer to the "why?" Why has the world been created?

The Christian does not deny that evolution has played an essential part in creation. The story in Genesis is a wonderful myth and the fact that reality does not correspond to it in detail does not detract from the rich insights it contains.

But the world took more than seven days to develop. It has taken billions of years and yet it remains a mystery of immense beauty and wonder. Even if God had not revealed himself, we would have to admit his existence by the very miracle of creation. Few people watching a beautiful sunset, hearing a Mozart symphony, experiencing the wonder of love, can fail to wonder whether there is a source which corresponds to all this human richness.

In fact God is not only a necessity to account for creation, but has also revealed himself in the Judaeo-Christian tradition ultimately in his only Son, Jesus Christ.

Through Jesus we have learned that God is a trinity of persons, the Father, the Son and the Spirit who relate to each other, in and through love. At the centre of the Godhead are persons in a relationship of love with each other. This God created the world out of love and relates to each one of us in a relationship of love. Furthermore, our relationship with one another, aiming to realise love, mirrors the life of God.

That is why human relationships are so important. Relationships of persons in and through love reflect the divine life and allow us to participate in it. As Catholics we recognise one such relationship as a sacrament, namely marriage. But all human relationships which have as their goal the realisation of love are sacraments in the wide sense in that, through relationships, we meet God in each other. It is this essential Christian belief that in our neighbour we encounter God that makes it essential we treat each other as persons of love and not as things. The object of personal relationships is to donate ourselves and receive the other. The object of things is to use them. Personal relationships are concerned with love and not with use and exploitation.

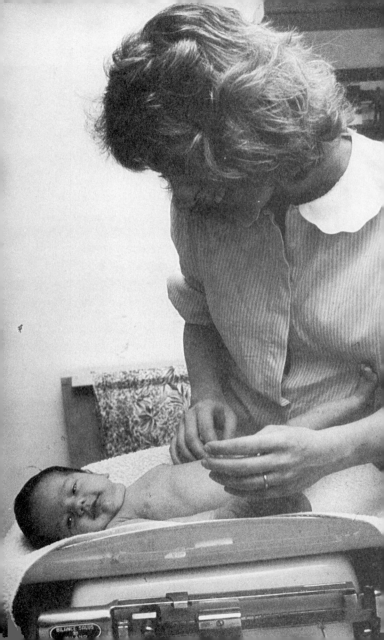

Chapter 2

The development
of the human personality

Psychologists tend to dwell on the early years of life. Most adults find this boring and want to concentrate on relationships in the here-and-now. This is perfectly understandable but how we relate currently is often influenced by our past experiences and so a certain amount of understanding of the early years is essential for the comprehension of current relationships.

The baby is born with the capacity to learn. It is programmed to be receptive to feelings and, later on, to the development of skills in its cognitive repertoire. In fact, human experience is built on the interaction between our innate capacities and what is offered to us by our parents. On this interaction the personality is built. For example, the baby has the capacity to suck, later on to chew and masticate and all it needs is milk from the breast and solid food. The baby is capable of smiling and it learns to imitate the smile of mother. It is capable of elimination and gradually learns to control its bowel and bladder. This learning is based on the innate response of the child to mother's initiatives. By and large the child responds positively when it is encouraged, approved and made to feel good and negatively when it is threatened, disapproved of and punished. This ability to learn when we are approved and appreciated persists and one of the essential features of relationship is to communicate approval and disapproval, which are the two ingredients that shape our whole life. At the opposite pole of approbation and affirmation lie criticism and fear. By and large we respond to praise much better than to punishment.

So the whole of childhood is a series of encounters between child and parent which prepares for adult relationships in which we repeat what we have learned as children. Our childhood is our first intimate relationship and our adulthood our second.

Many psychologists have given an outline of the essential emotional development of childhood. I have condensed a number of these in the following brief account.

The first year of life is critical for the survival of the child. It is utterly dependent on mother for its food and on the environment for its health. These two characteristics — food and healthy surroundings — remain vital for the rest of our lives.

In terms of feelings the baby is born and relies entirely on its mother for its survival. In order to achieve this, it forms an affective bond with her called emotional attachment. It does this by recognising her face and then the rest of her body. That is to say, it becomes familiar with her outline. Nobody else can replace her unique configuration. Secondly, the child recognises her voice and learns to respond distinctly to its tone and messages. Thirdly, mother holds the baby and touch becomes a powerful medium of intimacy. *This ability to form an attachment is the basis of all human relationships later on in life.* All our significant relationships need such attachments in which the person who matters to us is recognised by their unique physical and emotional make-up.

The second characteristic that the child learns in this first year is trust. In the process of being held, it experiences security in closeness. It feels safe, cared for and protected. This experience of trust is something that we all need to give and receive in all our relationships. It is the key of security and the basis on which relationships operate.

It is this fundamental trust between Jesus and his Father that formed the whole basis of his personality:

> Believe me that I am in the Father and the Father in me; or else believe me for the sake of the works themselves.
> (John 14:11)

Second and third years

During the second and third year the child learns to stand up, crawl, walk, dress, eat by itself and generally take charge of its life. It is a time punctuated by autonomy and a gradual separation between itself and mother. This process of autonomy is absolutely central in our relationships with one another. All our relationships like those of the toddler are a mixture of depending on others for some features of our survival, whilst we take care of ourselves in other respects. A balance between dependence and independence governs all relationships.

If the mother does not let go and allow the child to do its own thing, then she remains controlling and authoritarian and reduces the independence of the child. There are many such parents who have stifled their child's growth.

Another negative characteristic is to criticise constantly all the child tries to do. All its achievements are thus tainted with a sense of inadequacy and failure and it grows up feeling helpless.

As the child seeks its autonomy, there is often conflict between itself and its parents. Mother wants things done in a particular way and the child wants to do them in his own way. In the end mother yells or slaps. For a moment the child feels bad, the experience of guilt enters its life and it feels cut off. Very quickly there is reconciliation and forgiveness.

This pattern of behaviour, which is set down so early in life, remains with us until death. When we hurt or damage someone we love, we feel guilty and bad. We need forgiveness and reconciliation. In the same way, when others hurt us, we need to be reconciled and forgive them.

As already mentioned, the third year of life is the time when children can leave their mother and go to a play-group. The

child has learned to internalise mother, that is to say, preserve her in memory in her physical absence. This is an essential feature of all relationships. We cannot remain always in the physical presence of our spouse or friend. At regular intervals we have to leave them for short or long periods. But we can preserve them inside us.

This mechanism is fundamental for our relationship with God. We do not see, hear or touch God as the child hears the presence of its parents. What we do is build up a picture of a symbol we call God through the instruction of faith, prayers and religious education. We internalise God in us in this way and have a relationship with him.

Fourth and fifth year

These are the years when we begin to roam about, climb trees, to explore. We are constantly in trouble and we begin to experience feelings of shame. But at the same time we learn that we are fundamentally loved by experiencing recognition, feeling wanted and appreciated. The same applies to our adult relationships. Whilst we are always doing small things that can upset our relationship with each other, our basic belief is solidly based, that we are loveable and loved.

Whilst the child feels loveable and loved, it recognises nevertheless that there is an immense difference between itself and its parents. They are big, tall, clever, wise, strong and the child is aware of these things. This is a time when the child can feel envious of what parents have and the child has not.

Another feature of this period is jealousy. The young child is conscious that the parents have an intimate relationship and a triangular situation exists with the child feeling excluded. This is the famous Oedipus complex in which the young boy wants to possess mother and exclude father, and the young girl wants to possess father and exclude mother.

Both envy and jealousy are powerful emotions which can intrude in personal relationships.

School

At the age of five children start school. This is a time when the intensely personal, one-to-one relationship gives way to group experiences. The child learns to shape its life according to rules and regulations and form relationships with other children on a social basis.

It is a time of rapid intellectual progress and the worth of the person is measured by achievement. Whilst scholastic achievement is of immense importance, this is a critical period in the life of the child. During the next ten to fifteen years children have to learn that, however important work is, human relationships are even more important, otherwise the foundations are laid for an exclusive preoccupation with work at the expense of love in personal relationships.

Chapter 3

Adolescence

From about twelve years old the secondary sexual characteristics of boys and girls appear. This is the signal for a shift in interest from parents and relatives to young people of the opposite sex. Sexual attraction begins to play a significant role. The adolescent has three tasks to achieve. The first is the separation from parents into an autonomous individual. The second is the conclusion of school studies and either the beginning of work or higher education and the third is the sexual dimension.

Separation from parents

The growth towards maturity is a process of gradual separation between child and parents. As the young people develop physically, intellectually, socially and emotionally, they rely increasingly on themselves.

The decade between twelve and the early twenties is a time of a mixture of dependence and independence. The young person is still at home and has to follow the rules of the household and the expectations of parents and yet what he or she wants to communicate is that they are now adults who should have the freedom to run their own lives and to choose for themselves what they want. This is a situation laden with tension.

The manifestation of independence are shown in the way the young person wants to dress, the hours they keep, the activities they undertake and the resolute desire to pursue their own ideas. Some conflict between parents and adolescents is inevitable and yet most households negotiate this period without too much fuss.

Parents need to listen carefully to their children and allow room and space for experimentation. Mistakes will inevitably be made but, provided the parents remain flexible, they can allow their offspring to be self-reliant one minute and yet seek advice and help the next. So long as the parents respect the growing separateness of their child, the adolescent can feel safe to fluctuate between adulthood and childhood without losing face.

Work

By sixteen to eighteen the adolescent has finished school and is ready either for work or higher studies. Work with its financial independence brings a new dimension in the life of the person. This financial position not only requires the capacity to manage money but also allows the young man or woman to leave home and set up on their own. This is the ultimate destination of autonomy, living apart and earning one's own living.

There are problems at this stage. In the last years at school the adolescent was at the top of the school hierarchy. At work they start at the bottom. They may be unsure whether they can cope with the challenge, whether they will be liked by their colleagues and finally, whether they will enjoy the work they have undertaken.

Sexual attraction

The adolescent is a transformed person physically, with bodily contours that maximise their sexual appearance. Young men and women meet, talk, socialise, but all the time they are aware of each other as sexual beings. This sexual dimension is different for boys and girls.

Men are intensely preoccupied with physical appearance. Bodies are the centre of attraction. They want to have access to a beautiful girl, be with her, touch and explore her body and ultimately have intercourse with her. This final physical union is, of course, governed by social and religious rules but the desire to communicate physically is at its peak.

Girls also appreciate physical appearance but they are more concerned with the personality. They are orientated towards making a home and the qualities of kindness, understanding, tolerance, affection, tenderness, reliability play a major part in the exchange of sexual attraction.

A few men and women discover that they are not attracted to the opposite sex but their own. Such a homosexual orientation requires understanding and consideration as the necessary adjustment is made.

Confusion

It can be seen that the adolescent has a number of challenging tasks. They have to find their independence, assert it and yet remain in contact with their parents, establish themselves at work and feel confident with their sexuality to be able to attract and mingle with members of the opposite sex.

Sometimes all this communication is fraught with difficulties. There is a war with the parents and other figures of authority. Work is frightening and sexual relations are inhibited through the fear that one is not attractive enough.

Instead of normal development, there is confusion and uncertainty which takes the form of either staying at home, refusing to socialise or participating frantically in parties, consuming excessive alcohol, experimenting with drugs, behaving in a promiscuous manner in a desperate attempt to persuade oneself that all is well and one is attractive after all.

These excesses are rare but they can be part of the confusion of communicating clearly one's being. Such confusion needs encouragement and support to overcome the anxieties and realise the richness of potential which belongs to this phase of development.

Chapter 4

Marriage

Adolescence is a time when men and women socialise in groups. In the early twenties pairing begins to take place. This pairing is based on two experiences of communication: the first is social, called assortative mating, and the second is emotional which is described as falling in love.

Assortative mating

Despite the wide range of admixture in social groups, men and women pair with each other on the basis of similarity: that is to say, we meet a variety of people but we usually choose someone with a similar background in terms of intelligence, education, social class, ethnic group and tastes. This is called assortative mating which ensures, as far as possible, that we are capable or relating to each other on the basis of familiarity with each other's social world. We can share interests, tastes, level of awareness, orientation, goals, etc. and thus have a similar level of social communication.

Falling in love

Given that we choose someone from a similar background, this does not direct us to one individual person. We can fall in love with a number of possible choices. The ultimate choice still remains a mystery but it is influenced by physical appearance, in some instances by similarity of psychological traits such as gentleness, kindness, understanding, patience, tolerance or, in other instances, there is a complementarity as when an introvert marries an extrovert or a dominant personality marries a more dependent person.

The influence of the parents is also important. If our parental figures gave us a loving, affirmative experience, then we tend to choose someone similar. If our experiences were negative, we can repeat the pattern by choosing an equally impassive, dominant, rejecting figure but more often we select someone who has the opposite characteristics.

Thus, the final choice is made on a combination of conscious and unconscious factors based on appearance and similarity or complementarity or psychological traits, with parental experiences playing a part.

The period of falling in love is characterised by a heightened awareness of each other physically and emotionally. We want to spend as much time together as possible, exchange loving feelings in which we tell each other in extravagant terms how beautiful and attractive they are. Our tolerance of each other's limitations is at its highest and we put up with shortcomings that we would not accept from anyone else. Every part of our being is communicating affection and involvement and we look for a reciprocal giving of the other.

Loving

When we marry, we enter a commitment and the essence of our communication is to make ourselves available to each other in every possible way but specifically sexually. This commitment is life-long, exclusive and faithful and has as its purpose sustaining, healing and growth and the building of a family. In chapter 6 we shall consider the characteristics of sustaining, healing and growth; here I want to stress that at the heart of marriage is to be found life, the life of loving and new life.

The shift from falling in love to loving is the critical experience of marriage.

In our first intimate relationship of love between ourselves and parents we learned to associate attachment, trust, balance between dependence and independence, giving and receiving, the resolution of conflict, forgiveness and reconciliation with love. Marriage is the second intimate experience of life and loving is the exchange of the very same characteristics in-between a husband and wife as adults of equal worth. The viability of the marriage depends on the presence of this loving.

Sexual intercourse

This loving takes a special character when communicated through sexual intercourse. Sexual intercourse is a body language through which the couple express a variety of emotions. They affirm each other as persons as they signal to each other that they are the most important person in each other's life. They confirm each other's sexual identity. They can use coitus as a way of sealing forgiveness and forgetting the hurt they have caused each other. In the course of making love they give hope and thanks to each other for being the source of all their life.

Life

Thus sexual intercourse has the possibility of giving life to the couple and on some rare occasions *new* life. The use of sexual intercourse for conceiving a new life is very infrequent but once conceived the child needs love and stability and sexual intercourse allows the parents to experience both and in turn offer the child the security it needs.

Family

Thus marriage leads to a series of relationships of love, first between the parents, then between the parents and the children, between the children themselves and finally the whole family offers itself to others in its own community.

Chapter 5

Friendship

Everyone recognises the institution of marriage and everyone has friends but very little thought has been given to the meaning of friendship. We can start by describing three clear situations most of us experience in our life. The first is the series of relationships we have at work, society, in a club or a committee. Here we have distinct roles to play in relationship to the other members of the organisation. These are not friends or relatives but acquaintances. Next we have friends and, finally, in the family we have relatives.

Perhaps one way of appreciating friendship is to look at the relationship between our Lord and his apostles:

> This is my commandment, that you love one another as I have loved you. Greater love has no man than this, that a man lay down his life for his friends. You are my friends if you do what I command you. No longer do I call you servants, for the

servant does not know what his master is doing; but I have called you friends, for all that I have heard from my Father I have made known to you.

(John 15:12-15)

What characterises friendship as we see it in our Lord?

Revelation

At the heart of friendship lies revelation of our inner world to another person. Jesus revealed himself as the Son of the Father, the core of his identity. What we reveal about ourselves is governed by the quality of relationship we have with each other. Friends reveal their minds and feelings and share social activity but not their bodies, that is something preserved for marriage.

Trust

We reveal ourselves fully to our friends in the hope and certainty that we shall be understood and received completely. We all long to be known and fully appreciated. Our Lord revealed himself completely to the apostles with the certain knowledge that ultimately they would grasp who he was. This they did and established a Church to preserve his continuous presence.

Affection

As we reveal ourselves and long for understanding, we also want tenderness, affection and kindness. This is not to say that our friends don't get cross with us; they certainly do. Remember how angry Our Lord was at times with Peter, his most trusted friend. But generally we expect a degree of appreciation and affirmation that makes us feel complete and special.

Sacrifice

Our Lord tells us that to lay down one's life for a friend is a great act of sacrificial love and he did precisely that for us. Normally we do not die for our friends but it is characteristic of friendship that we make sacrifices for them.

Enduring

The difference between roles in ordinary relationships and deep friendships is that the latter are enduring. Friendship is characterised by a continuity in which no matter how long is the time interval since we saw our friend last, we can resume a deep encounter immediately because the sense of belonging and mattering to each other has never been suspended.

Friendship and marriage

There is a close association between friendship and marriage in the sense that in both relationships there is a sharing of loving feelings. But in marriage there is a physical sexual dimension which is unique to it. Both in friendship and marriage there is recalled and relived the foundations of love learned in childhood with parents.

Chapter 6

Sustaining, healing and growth

Human relationships have a deeper layer of engagement which is not superficially obvious but nevertheless remains fundamental both for marriage and friendship. In my various writings I have designated this level of interaction as sustaining, healing and growth and I will describe briefly these terms.

Sustaining

At the very centre of our being is the reality of living. For this we need a material dimension, that is food, clothes, house, job and money, which is the external sustaining and an internal sustaining in which we feel continuously recognised, wanted and appreciated as a person of worth and value.

The material sustaining is what married couples give to each other as they share the provision of their household. As friends we support each other materially and socially when someone is in need, and we try to do the same for the poor in our own country and those in need overseas. There is no point in proclaiming external love when your spouse or friend is dying of hunger.

Having established material sustaining, we then have to address ourselves to the social, intellectual and emotional sustaining of each other. In brief, that means that we need to be available socially and reassured that we are right and good in what we think, feel and do.

The largest part of intimate exchange is a process whereby we reveal ourselves and in making contact we want to be reassured about our reasoning, feelings and the righteousness of our acts. We need to reveal and be known in such a way that we are affirmed.

Healing

In the course of our upbringing all of us sustain wounds. These wounds are inflicted in two ways. The first is through our genes. We know that genes can influence mood and make men and women anxious or depressed. Secondly, wounds are inflicted through the upbringing we received from our parents. As a result of this combination of genes and parents we may grow up feeling inadequate, lacking confidence, security, feeling unloveable and unwanted, coupled with moodiness and misery.

Both in marriage and friendship, spouses and friends can give their partner a second opportunity. Someone who is confident can give those lacking this a sense of their own worth. Those who feel rejected can come to feel unconditionally accepted. Men and women hungry for love and affection can receive it through undivided attention of their friend or spouse and in this way feel fulfilled for the first time. Those who feel misunderstood can be listened to with care and given the feeling of being taken seriously. In this way wounded people can be given continuous and intense attention which gives them a correcting experience.

Healing lies at the heart of the Christian faith whose members are constantly seeking the wholeness of the creator. This wholeness is not achieved instantly. It is realised slowly through healing personal relationships.

Growth

It has been shown repeatedly that the human personality develops gradually by acquiring its potential through the stages of its development and functioning in an autonomous way. We all function by a combination of self-reliance and personal initiative. But this self-reliance takes time to fully develop.

When we marry or establish a deep friendship, we may still be dependent on our spouse or friend for guidance, advice, support, encouragement, reassurance and, indeed, they may do things such as driving for us, taking care of our finances, choosing holidays for us. With the passage of time we develop a deeper sense of confidence. We want to do things like driving, choosing our holidays, the clothes we buy, entirely by ourselves without advice or having it done for us. This is a process of gradual growth into independence and it is something that goes on our whole life.

The friend or spouse who has given us the support to go on growing is like a parental figure who rejoices at our achievement. They are proud of what we can do and we in turn put our newly-discovered skills at their service.

Growth is not only confined to independence. With the passage of time we begin to realise and appreciate more deeply the way our spouse or friend functions as a person. We recognise their sensitivities and we try not only to avoid hurting them by teasing them, challenging them, making fun of them but we give them the support they need to overcome their difficulties. This is particularly important in matters which lead to conflict. When our spouse or friend shouts at us, we need to pay heed to their cry of pain. The whole point about conflict is to recognise the wound we are re-opening and not only to avoid doing that but also to make an effort to help them overcome their wound. People can be sensitive about their appearance, intelligence, skills, etc. Instead of criticising them we should try to affirm them by showing them how talented they are and in this way build up their confidence.

In short, there is an infinite possibility of increasing our loving by reducing our criticism and enlarging our appreciation and affirmation.

Chapter 7

Self-esteem

We have all grown up with a deep sense that it is wrong to be selfish, egocentric, taking pride in our achievements. We have been taught that pride is dangerous and humility is good. But there is a vast difference between being proud and selfish and feeling loveable and good. There is such a thing as love of self which psychologists call self-esteem.

Self-esteem is fundamental for human communication. If we don't feel loveable, then we cannot believe that anyone wants to know us, form a relationship with us or love us. There are many such men and women who cannot accept themselves and feel they are worth nothing. They are the loners of this world who cannot form relationships. Every time someone tries to approach them they either depart instantly or they remain hopefully around until the other makes overtures of closeness and appreciation and then they run away from the signals of being wanted and appreciated.

So that feeling loveable is the key to allowing other people to get near us and it reflects our ability to accept the appreciative feelings of others.

Self-esteem not only reflects feeling loveable but also feeling good. If we feel good, then we trust ourselves to have the ability to offer good things to others. If we feel empty and saturated with badness, then we don't feel we have anything of value to give others.

Self-esteem is absolutely central in the exchange between persons. Spouses can go on showering love on us and so can friends but what we tolerate, receive and accept depends ultimately on how loveable we feel.

Although love of self is a difficult concept for all of us — but particularly Christians, whose sense of sin, guilt and unworthiness can often be a penetrating experience — nevertheless we can take heart from our Lord who was not afraid to put himself on an equal footing with the Father and to feel loved by him.

Our Lord's ability to feel loveable, like all of us, depended on a very positive and affirmative childhood in which he felt loved unconditionally by Mary and Joseph. But we have an example of his heavenly Father's affirmation at his baptism.

> And when Jesus was baptised, he went up immediately from the water, and behold, the heavens were opened and he saw the Spirit of God descending like a dove, and alighting on him; and lo, a voice from heaven saying, "This is my beloved Son, with whom I am well pleased."
>
> (Matthew 3:16-17)

Such an experience of unconditional acceptance must have been a powerful source of Jesus' self-esteem. Such love of self has nothing to do with pride or selfishness but is based on a reality of possessing all our gifts and feeling good about them. By this I mean that we have access to our body, mind, feelings and, without exaggerating their worth, we do not underestimate them either. Genuine self-esteem is based on a realistic assessment of our own capacity and worth.

Jesus had such a powerful conviction of his own identity and such a high degree of self-esteem that he was not afraid to place himself on the same footing as the Father:

> Do you not believe that I am in the Father and the Father in me? The

words that I say to you I do not speak on my own authority; but the Father who dwells in me does his works.

(John 14:10)

Chapter 8

Difficulties
in relationships

The reader may say that it is alright for
our Lord to be full of self-esteem; he was
after all the Son of God. But we are not
in the same league. This is not true.
Through Baptism we are incorporated in
the life of Christ and we have the potential to be almost as rich as he was in the
fulness of his being.

In reality, of course, we are all wounded
people with our own limitations. Our
relationships suffer from a whole variety
of disadvantages.

Intimacy

We long for closeness and yet we may
be threatened by it. We may feel in the
presence of other people that they take
over our lives, dominate and organise us
and ignore our own specific contribution. If our self-esteem is low, we are sur-
prised that anyone wants to get close to
us and we find it very hard to believe we
are loveable. The Christian who believes

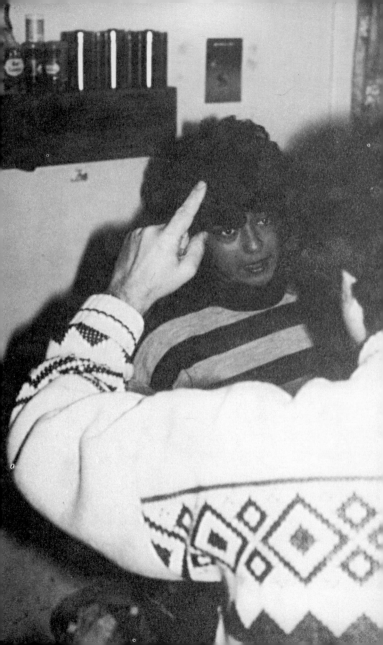

that God loves them but cannot feel loved by their neighbour has a difficulty to overcome here.

Revelation

Even though we feel close to another person we may not feel it possible to tell them about ourselves. Deep inside us there is a sense of shame and guilt about our life. We are sure that if we reveal the details of our hostile or sexual feelings we shall be rejected. The fear of rejection makes us secretive and we continue to entertain our painful thoughts instead of revealing them to those who love us.

If our self-esteem is low, we believe that we are the ones who have something to hide. Instead we should appreciate that all of us are in the same position. Nobody is perfect. Our imperfections are matched by those of others and we should not hide them.

Anger

If our self-esteem is low we feel vulnerable, sensitive to criticism and rejection and over the years we build powerful defences to protect our insecurity. When others criticise us, we retaliate with anger, aggression and hostility. If we feel taunted by our accusers, we want to destroy them. These thoughts bring many feelings of guilt and we can spend our lives hovering between our anger and guilt.

Envy and jealousy

When we feel secure in ourselves we are not threatened by others. The advantages others have do not taunt us with our limitations. If we feel insecure, then we are envious of others. We want to have their money, strength, looks, status, authority and power. We will do anything to become like them and, if they stand in our way, we can try to eliminate them through all the means available to us. The envious person, lacking the feeling of worth, gets their sense of value from the discomfort of others. When others are defeated, humiliated or embarrassed, then the unsure person feels good.

Envy and jealousy are closely linked. When we are unsure about our worth we live constantly with the feeling that someone will come and take away our friend or spouse. The man who smiles at our spouse at a party is a threat and we harangue our partner for smiling back.

Anxiety and guilt

Thus, at the centre of our marked relationships lies the continuous anxiety that at any moment we shall be made redundant, rejected or supplanted. Our feelings of lack of self-esteem and insecurity make us angry and guilty and we spend our whole life hovering between uncertainty and self-rejection.

Reality and love

The reality is that none of us is as bad as we think we are. Often we exaggerate our limitations and we need a loving partner, friend or wise counsellor to remind us of our true value. This is what loving relationships achieve for us, a combination of healing and restoring our worth and dignity.

God, me and my neighbour

But finally we have to remember that Jesus did not come to rescue the rich or the perfect. He came to offer his love to the wounded. He gave his life for sin, that is to say all that is imperfect and incomplete. He died for each one of us who is imperfect and incomplete.

We cannot see or touch God but we believe in faith that we are in the presence of God in our relationship with each other. Our neighbour, whether they be our spouse, relative or friend, is the person who stands for Jesus.

Relationships of love sustain, heal and allow us to grow and in doing so we participate here and now in the constant relationship of love of the Trinity.

We were born out of love for love, a love that is fulfilled fully in heaven. Human relationships of love are a foretaste of this heaven.

DISCUSSION STARTERS
by
Maureen McCollum

PERSONAL

In the context of this booklet, these questions are intended to pinpoint certain facets of communication and human relationships so that our strengths and weaknesses will come to light enabling us to build on what is good and work on the less acceptable aspects of communication in everyday living.

1. Write down your earliest memory.

   Look at it for a while in silence.

   Do you think it had any effect on your life? In your experience of loving?

2. Write down five happy occasions.

   Look at them for a while in silence, remembering.

   How did they affect your life and your relationships with others and with God?

3. Write down the areas of your greatest difficulty in communicating, with others/with God.

   Look at them for a while in silence and try to discover *why* these areas are difficult for you.

4. Write down the areas where you think you communicate well.

Look at them for a while in silence and try to discover *why* you find them easy, productive, satisfying, etc.

Arising from these questions write down three strong points and three weak points you notice about yourself in the area of interpersonal communication and loving.

Look at them in silence for a while and work out what you want to do about them.

GROUP

1. Discuss the relationships of people in a television programme of your choice, e.g. Dallas, Dynasty, Eastenders, Coronation Street, a comedy show, etc. Do you notice people around you who behave like these fictitious characters?

Do you find they mirror, even dimly, some of your own relationships?

Why do you think these programmes are so popular?

Do they reflect your experiences of loving?

2. Would each one in the group suggest a necessary ingredient for good communication in the following areas:

family • work or study • people in general • authority.

Look at these ingredients and try to discover what hinders them from being effective.

3. Can you think of someone you would rate as a good communicator? a public figure and someone close to you. What is it that makes him/her such a good communicator?

4. We often hear that someone has a "good relationship" with someone else. We probably feel that we have a good relationship in our lives. What makes it "good" for you? Does it come naturally or has it to be worked on by you or by the other person?

5. Once relationships are established, how can we maintain them and renew them?

6. What are the difficulties in loving?